He was not of an age, but for all time...

Jane Purcell

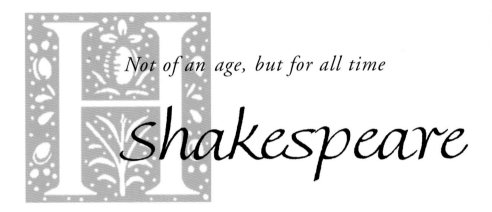

Not of an age, but for all time

Shakespeare

AT THE HUNTINGTON

HUNTINGTON LIBRARY ❦ SAN MARINO

ISBN-10:0-87328-201-9
ISBN-13:978-0-87328-201-7

HUNTINGTON LIBRARY PRESS
DIRECTOR: Peggy Park Bernal
EDITOR: Susan Green
PRODUCTION COORDINATOR: Jean Patterson
DESIGNER: Lilli Colton
PHOTOGRAPHY: Huntington Library Photo
Services Department (John Sullivan, Senior
Photographer; Manuel Flores, Photographer;
Devonne Tice, Library Assistant-Digital
Imaging)
COPY EDITOR: Carol Pearson
INDEX: Ellen Brink
PICTURE RESEARCH: Genevieve Preston
Printed and Bound by CS Graphics

ENDPAPERS: Watercolors from the "Travel
Album of Hieronymous Tielsch" by Servatius
Reichell (1603–16). Seventeen sketches, of
which eight are reproduced here, provide a
glimpse into the world in which Shakespeare
lived and wrote.
FRONT: James I bodyguard; a London merchant's
wife; a noble lady on horseback; a London
water carrier; Lady Mayoress of London
BACK: An English lord's servant; a lady of high
rank riding in a coach; costume of a lady of
high rank

LIBRARY OF CONGRESS CATALOGING-IN-PUBLICATION DATA

Purcell, Jane, 1954–
    Not of an age, but for all time : Shakespeare at the Huntington / by Jane Purcell.
        p. cm.
    Includes bibliographical references and index.
        1. Shakespeare, William, 1564–1616—Library resources. 2. Shakespeare, William, 1564–1616—Bibliography.
3. Library resources—California—San Marino. 4. Henry E. Huntington Library and Art Gallery. 5. Rare
books—California—San Marino. I. Henry E. Huntington Library and Art Gallery. II. Title.
    Z8811.P87 2004
    [PR2894]
    822.3'3—dc22
                    2004018020

Table of Contents

Introduction

...Soule of the Age!
The applause! delight! the wonder of our Stage!
My Shakespeare, rise; I will not lodge thee by
Chaucer, or Spenser, or bid Beaumont lye
A little further, to make thee a roome:
Thou art a Moniment, without a tombe,
And art alive still, while thy Booke doth live,
And we have wits to read, and praise to give.
That I not mixe thee so, my braine excuses;
I meane with great, but disproportion'd Muses:
For, if I thought my judgement were of yeeres,
I should commit thee surely with thy peeres,
And tell, how farre thou didstst [sic] our Lily out-shine,
Or sporting Kid, or Marlowes mighty line.
And though thou hadst small Latine, and lesse Greeke,
From thence to honour thee, I would not seeke
For names; but call forth thund'ring Æschilus,
Euripides, and Sophocles to us...
....
He was not of an age, but for all time...

—EXCERPT FROM "TO THE MEMORY OF MY
BELOVED, THE AUTHOR MR. WILLIAM SHAKESPEARE,"
BEN JONSON IN THE FIRST FOLIO, 1623

"Knock, knock! Who's there?" debuted not in a child's riddle, but in act 2 of *Macbeth*. The English language is rich with words and phrases we owe to Shakespeare. "Brave new world," "fair play," "foul play," and "too much of a good thing" are just a handful of household examples. In fact, that very expression "household words" comes to us from *Henry V*. William Shakespeare was an unparalleled master at coining new words and phrases.

The Huntington Library contains one of the richest collections in the world of Shakespeare's writings in the original published editions. One needn't have the collector's passion for books or a knowledge of academic jargon to find the Huntington's Shakespeare collection fascinating. This book focuses on some of the more important of Henry E. Huntington's acquisitions in terms of understanding Shakespeare, with special emphasis on quarto copies of the plays published in Shakespeare's lifetime. The illustrations are from the Huntington's library and art collections—many of them from a huge extra-illustrated set of Shakespeare's plays compiled by Thomas Turner in the mid-nineteenth century and acquired by Huntington in 1917.

OPPOSITE: This monument to Shakespeare in Stratford's Holy Trinity Church was installed a few years after his death.

Henry E. Huntington: The Collector and Connoisseur

> Keep me, I pray, in wisdom's way
> That I may truths eternal seek;
> I need protecting care to-day,—
> My purse is light, my flesh is weak.
> So banish from my erring heart
> All baleful appetites and hints
> Of Satan's fascinating art,
> Of first editions, and of prints.
> Direct me in some godly walk
> Which leads away from bookish strife,
> That I with pious deed and talk
> May extra-illustrate my life.
>
> —EUGENE FIELD 1850–95
> "THE BIBLIOMANIAC'S PRAYER,"
> 1ST STANZA

Railroad and real estate developer Henry Edwards Huntington (1850–1927) was a collector without equal who assembled world-class collections of rare books and manuscripts, works of art, and plants.

OPPOSITE: Henry Edwards Huntington in 1924.

In his twenties he joined the railroad enterprises of his uncle Collis P. Huntington, one of the "Big Four" of the California railroads. In San Francisco, he shared with his uncle the management of the Southern Pacific Company, a holding company for the Southern and Central Pacific railroads. Collis Huntington died in 1900. In 1902, Henry Huntington withdrew from the management of the Southern Pacific, moved to Los Angeles, and bought the San Marino ranch.

There he organized the interurban railway system, which provided quick, efficient, and inexpensive transportation throughout the greater Los Angeles area. He was the largest single landowner in Southern California at the time, having acquired tracts of land for urban and suburban development. He was involved in local agriculture and industry, the hotel business, and many leading social and civic organizations. As a philanthropist, he donated land for parks and schools and provided money to various youth organizations. To enrich the intellectual life, he supported local colleges and founded the institution that bears his name. He was frequently lauded as a hero for his many contributions to the development of the Los Angeles area.

The Library, designed by Myron Hunt, was built in 1920 to house Huntington's growing collection of books and manuscripts.

In 1910, at the age of sixty, Huntington sold the interurban system so he could concentrate more completely on his lifelong love of books. He bought rare manuscripts and first editions at a rapid rate, sometimes purchasing entire libraries, occasionally at record prices. The books were assembled in New York where Mr. Huntington had a large apartment. As soon as the library building was completed in San Marino in 1921, railroad cars of books began to arrive at the ranch, where they were catalogued and made available for study by scholars.

Huntington began collecting art in 1907, choosing to specialize in British portraits of the Georgian period by such artists as Thomas Gainsborough, Joshua Reynolds, and Sir Thomas Lawrence. He was advised and encouraged by Arabella Huntington, the widow of Collis. They spent many hours together after Collis's death, settling his estate. They were married in 1913. In 1919 they signed an indenture that transferred their San Marino property and collections to a non-profit educational trust, founding the three-part institution that we know today. Arabella died in 1924 and Henry in 1927. They are interred in the mausoleum on the 206-acre estate near Los Angeles.

COLLECTING SHAKESPEARE

As Huntington became more knowledgeable, discriminating, and wealthy, he was eager and able to outbid many of his rivals for original and early editions of Shakespeare's works until his collection was one of the four largest in the world. Each of these four collections is vast, but none is complete. Huntington was a true collector. Though seldom motivated by the desire to have one more of something, he kept an eye and an ear out for a better copy, version, or edition of a rare work.

"You can't have everything," the joke goes. "Where would you put it?" But space wasn't a deterrent for Huntington. He approached collecting rare books and manuscripts, art, and exotic plants for his garden with the same passion and ambition with which he had earlier acquired large tracts of land for urban and suburban development. He bought so many entire libraries that his collection was known as the "library of libraries." Huntington's acquisition of the E. D. Church library in 1911, purchased for a reputed $750,000, included twelve Shakespeare folios and thirty-seven quartos, plus rare first editions of Spenser and Milton. The purchase of the duke of Devonshire's collection of plays in 1914, the F. R. Halsey collection in 1915, and the Bridgewater library in 1917 brought together twenty-nine copies of the folio editions of Shakespeare's plays, as many as seventy-three quartos printed before 1641, and most of the earliest editions of his nondramatic poems.

"Men prize the thing ungain'd more than it is," wrote Shakespeare in *Troilus and Cressida* (1.2.289).[1] Collections unite those who love the same thing, but they also create rivals for limited treasure. With his acquisitions Huntington nosed out his chief competitors for these rarities, the British Museum (now the British Library) in London and the Bodleian Library at Oxford. The Bodleian began with a definite advantage since, as early as 1611, London publishers were required to donate a copy of each new book to the library named for Sir Thomas Bodley, who had re-endowed it in 1602. But Huntington refused to be hampered by his "late start." He also went toe-to-toe, so to speak, with his American rival Henry Clay Folger, who bid for many of the same quartos and folios for what would become the Folger Shakespeare Library in Washington, D.C.[2]

Huntington's competitive glee can be glimpsed in a note from August 1914 to his librarian George Watson Cole, written just after acquiring eleven volumes from the collection of Marsden Perry, a fellow railroad developer:

These books I will bring home with me when I return. It is necessary that nothing should be said of this transaction for some time. It makes quite a reduction in the number of plays I have to secure to be even with the British Museum.[3]

That an American library, and eventually a California library at that, could match the collections of the two great libraries of England was a source of considerable pride to Huntington.

For almost three centuries before Huntington sold his interurban railway system (1910) to concentrate on his book collection, Shakespeare had already played a defining role in American culture. The Pilgrims came to Plymouth in 1620—three years before the publication of the First Folio. "Had [the plays] been published earlier, our forefathers, or the most poetical of them, might have stayed home to read them," mused Ralph Waldo Emerson in 1864. But it wasn't necessary to live in England to enjoy the plays. In 1730, an amateur production of *Romeo and Juliet* in New York City became the first recorded production of a play by Shakespeare in the New World. In 1751, the London Company of Comedians landed in Virginia and made its way through the lower colonies performing *Richard III, King Lear, Romeo and Juliet, Othello,* and *Hamlet.* George Washington saw one of their performances in Williamsburg.

Alexis de Tocqueville, an aristocratic Frenchman who came to the United States in 1831, noted the popularity of Shakespeare across the nation: "There is hardly a pioneer's hut that does not contain a few odd volumes of Shakespeare." Abraham Lincoln's formative reading consisted mainly of the King James Bible, Blackstone's lectures on English law, and Shakespeare. In 1863, he wrote to the actor James Hackett: "Some of Shakespeare's Plays, I have never read, whilst others I have gone over perhaps as frequently as any unprofessional reader. Among the latter are *Lear, Richard Third, Henry Eighth, Hamlet,* and especially *Macbeth.* I think none equals *Macbeth.*" In 1879, Walt Whitman, the most American of poets, recalled the first time he had seen Lincoln passing through New York: "He look'd with curiosity upon that immense sea of faces, and the sea of faces return'd the look with similar curiosity. In both there was a dash of comedy, almost farce, such as Shakespeare puts in his blackest tragedies."

From the eighteenth century onward, authors—including quintessentially American writers like Mark Twain—have drawn on Shakespeare in a variety of ways. The actor Charles Kean began his Shakespeare tour in 1831 in New York and eventually returned fifteen years later through the Mississippi Valley. Mark Twain depicts Huckleberry Finn traveling along the Mississippi River with a pair of rogues who try to pass themselves off as Shakespearean actors. Nathaniel Hawthorne said of Shakespeare, "There is no exhausting the various interpretation of his symbols; and a thousand years hence, a world of new readers will possess a whole library of new books, as we ourselves do, in these volumes old already" (*Our Old Home*, 1863).

The Shakespeare bookcase, a curiosity made from timbers of 40 different buildings associated with Shakespeare's life or mentioned in his plays.

Mr. WILLIAM
SHAKESPEARES

COMEDIES,
HISTORIES, &
TRAGEDIES.

Publiſhed according to the True Originall Copies.

Martin Droeshout ſculpſit London.

LONDON

Printed by Iſaac Iaggard, and Ed. Blount. 1623.

shakespeare the Man

What is a man,
If his chief good and market of his time
Be but to sleep and feed? a beast, no more.
Sure He that made us with such large discourse,
Looking before and after, gave us not
That capability and godlike reason
To fust in us unus'd.

—*HAMLET* (4.4.33–39)

The search for the historical William Shakespeare can be both frustrating and addictive. Although many biographies have been written about Shakespeare, the facts are sparse, and his life remains stubbornly private. The date of his birth was not recorded, but he was baptized at Holy Trinity Church in Stratford-on-Avon, England, on Wednesday, April 26, 1564. Because the church required that baptisms be performed within a few days of birth, it is customary to celebrate his birthday on April 23 (St. George's Day), the same date on which he died fifty-two years later in 1616. His parents were John and Mary Shakespeare, and William was the oldest of six surviving children. The couple's first two children died as infants. John Shakespeare was a glover (someone who makes gloves), as well as a member of the town council and later a bailiff and an alderman. He appears to have been a respected and popular man. Mary Shakespeare was born Mary Arden, the youngest of eight daughters born to a gentleman farmer, a wealthy man whose family can be traced back prior to the Norman Conquest. She was raised about three miles from Stratford.

Although there is no written evidence that Shakespeare attended King Edward VI's New School, it is supposed that he did. He was, after all, the son of one of Stratford's most prominent citizens. He probably saw his first plays in Stratford performed by troupes of traveling actors. There is no record of the young William's courtship of Anne Hathaway, who was eight years older than he, but they did marry in 1582, and the union did produce three children: Susanna in 1583, and the twins Hamnet and Judith in 1585.

We don't really know why Shakespeare left his family to make a living in London, but leave them he did, at some point during the period of time biographers often refer to as "the lost years." It's easy to assume that he left to become an actor, but from a document in the Folger Library we learn that his first known London address was in Westminster, not particularly near the playhouses.[4] Whatever his motivation for moving to the city, he did become an actor, and sometime before 1592 he began writing plays as well. He wrote thirty-eight of them before returning to Stratford in 1611 and retiring with his wife, thus closing a successful and lucrative

OPPOSITE: First Folio (1623) title page features this well-known portrait of Shakespeare by Martin Droeshout.

career. He died five years later and is buried in the chancel of Holy Trinity Church. On the slab over the grave appear the words:

GOOD FRIEND FOR JESUS SAKE FORBEARE,

TO DIGG THE DUST ENCLOSED HEARE.

BLESTE BE Y^E MAN Y^t SPARES THESE STONES.

AND CURST BE HE Y^t MOVES MY BONES.

By the time of his death William Shakespeare was a man of considerable property, and his will suggests he took great pains to entail this property to a much hoped-for male heir. Unfortunately his only son, Hamnet, died in 1596 at the age of eleven. Hamnet's twin sister, Judith, had three sons. The oldest was born only a few months after her father's death, and she named him Shakespeare, but he died in infancy. The other two barely made it to adulthood, and when Judith died at the age of seventy-seven, she had long outlived all three sons. Susanna, the oldest daughter, gave Shakespeare the only grandchild he ever knew: Elizabeth. When Elizabeth died childless in 1670, the direct line of descent ended.

In short, when Shakespeare writes in *A Midsummer Night's Dream*, "The actors are at hand; and, by their show / You shall know all, that you are like to know" (5.1.116–17), he might just as well be teasing us about his biography, since it is, indeed, primarily through his plays that we come to know him.

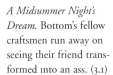

A Midsummer Night's Dream. Bottom's fellow craftsmen run away on seeing their friend transformed into an ass. (3.1)

Romeo and Juliet. Romeo tells Juliet he must leave Verona or risk death. (3.5)

Some find it curious that Shakespeare showed so great an interest in what became of the property he had amassed, but so little interest in publishing the plays that earned him his immortal reputation. It is highly probable that Shakespeare saw himself as an actor first and a writer second. Plays have their life on the stage, and Shakespeare was a team player who wrote plays because his acting company (the Lord Chamberlain's Men for most of his career, renamed "the King's Men" when they gained James's patronage) badly needed successful plays to stay competitive. Life as an actor was not an easy one in Elizabethan England. Ben Jonson, a contemporary playwright, began as an actor but gave up acting as soon as he could make a living with his pen. However, even after he began writing plays, Shakespeare never gave up acting until he retired from the theater. Actors continually attest to the fact that only another actor with an understanding of the necessity of clear delivery of lines, breath control, and emphasis could have written Shakespeare's plays, which were very much meant to be acted and not to be read. This may explain why the hearts of high school students often sink at the assigned reading of *Julius Caesar, Macbeth, Romeo and Juliet, Hamlet,* and

OPPOSITE: Hamlet
encounters the ghost of
his father. (1.4)

A Midsummer Night's Dream (the five plays most likely to be a student's
first introduction to Shakespeare in the United States).[5] But if these same
students have the good fortune to see a production, most will, if somewhat grudgingly at first, become fans, perhaps for life. Even an uneven
production of a Shakespeare play is bound to yield moments of magic.
Shakespeare's Hamlet expresses great confidence in the power of the theater when he says:

> *...I have heard*
> *That guilty creatures sitting at a play*
> *Have by the very cunning of the scene*
> *Been strook so to the soul, that presently*
> *They have proclaim'd their malefactions.* (2.2.588–92)

The survival of this poetic magic is due in part to the plague. The
Black Death that closed down the London theaters from 1592 to 1594 not
only encouraged writers such as Shakespeare to try other kinds of writing,
but also encouraged theater companies to sell their existing scripts to
printers who sold them to a "reading" public.

In Elizabethan England no play could be performed until it was
licensed by the Master of the Revels, who determined that it contained no
seditious material—that is, content that maligned the government.
Obviously a script had to be written before it could be licensed, and since
nothing could be added to a play after it was licensed, these written versions might be longer than what actually appeared on the stage.

After a play was licensed (for which a fee was charged), the theater
company would work on the licensed script, reducing it to two or three
hours of performance time. The next expense was probably a payment to
a copyist to write out the actors' parts. The only document of this kind
that has survived is one made for Edward Alleyn, with corrections in
Alleyn's handwriting.[6] Alleyn, a contemporary of Shakespeare, was a leading tragedian.

Plays that proved popular on the stage might eventually be sold to a
printer and published, but theater companies were anxious to protect
their rights to their plays from the very beginning. In order to do this, a
company would have its plays licensed by the Worshipful Company of
Stationers, the English printers' guild or trade organization, where, for a
fee, the titles of the plays were entered into the Stationers' Register by date,
effectively providing a copyright even before the plays were produced.

"Seven Ages of Man" from *As You Like It* (2.7). Jacques, the melancholy satirist, gives voice to Shakespeare's most famous theatrical metaphor.

TOP, LEFT TO RIGHT: Infant in the nurse's arms; Whining schoolboy; The lover, sighing like a furnace.

BOTTOM, LEFT TO RIGHT: The soldier, full of strange oaths; The justice in fair round belly; Old age in lean and slippered pantaloons; Second childhood, *sans teeth, sans eyes, sans taste, sans every thing.*

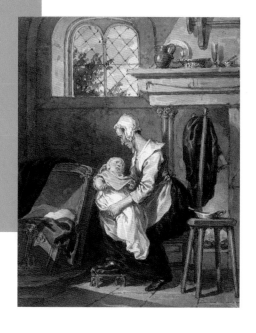

Shakespeare Studies at the Huntington

Take him and cut him out in little stars,
And he will make the face of heaven so fine
That all the world will be in love with night,
And pay no worship to the garish sun.
—*ROMEO AND JULIET* (3.2.22–25)

*P*eople who love the plays don't always love the scholars, but the scholars love the Huntington, and we owe a great deal of what we know about Shakespeare to their careful and diligent work.

Before we move on, a word about publishing terms: What is a folio? A quarto? Both are ways of referring to a book by its general size. In Shakespeare's time, all paper was handmade sheet by sheet on various-sized rectangular molds averaging about twenty inches long. Large books were produced by folding each of these sheets once, across the middle of the longer side, creating two leaves (four pages) from each sheet—like a modern newspaper. Any book in this format was called a folio (the Latin word for "leaf"). Lengthy scholarly works and collected works of an author were often issued "in folio." The next size down was a quarto, in which the sheets were folded twice, so that each leaf was a quarter of a whole sheet. An Elizabethan quarto was about half as tall as a modern magazine, and this was a normal format for shorter individual works, including plays. Even smaller formats—octavo, duodecimo—were also in common use.

The outstanding strength of the Huntington's Shakespeare collection is in editions of the plays published individually in quarto during the author's lifetime. Eighteen of Shakespeare's plays (from among the thirty-eight now commonly regarded as the body of his work) appeared separately before he died, in a total of forty-two editions. Of these editions, the Huntington owns thirty-five, not counting second copies and variants.

In 1623, seven years after Shakespeare's death, thirty-six of his plays were collected in folio format, known as the First Folio. This edition, published by his actor friends John Heminge and Henry Condell, is important because it prints eighteen of the plays—almost half of his known total output—for the first time. For some of the others it gives a text that scholars believe to be closer to what Shakespeare actually wrote than the quarto version. Further folio editions appeared in 1632, 1664, and 1685. The Huntington collection includes four copies of the First Folio, ten of the second, seven of the third, and eight of the fourth.

OPPOSITE: The folio (BOTTOM) and quarto editions of Shakespeare's works differ in size as well as content.

And why do these quartos and folios matter? Since there are no surviving manuscripts of Shakespeare's plays, the early printed texts form the basis for scholarly criticism, providing the essential clues to what Shakespeare said, wrote, or intended. For instance, when Hamlet dies, are his last words "Farewel Horatio, heaven receive my soule" as printed in the first quarto (Q1)? Or are they "the rest is silence," with Horatio replying "…good night sweete Prince / And flights of Angels sing thee to thy rest" as printed in the second quarto (Q2)? This kind of question can be repeated almost endlessly for every Shakespeare play for which there is more than one early edition with any authority.

Although the value of a copy of a play printed in the lifetime of the author would seem to be very high, there are circumstances that make some of the quartos of Shakespeare's plays published in his lifetime seem corrupt and therefore less authentic. Beginning with Alfred W. Pollard in 1909,[7] some scholars have used the terms "bad quarto" and "good quarto" to differentiate between early editions. A quarto has been called bad when scholars have suspected that it is a copy of a play that has been seriously flawed in the process of its transmission from what Shakespeare may have written to its printed form. Some quarto editions of plays differ so much from other versions and the differences seem to produce such inferior readings that scholars have theorized that they were constructed from memory—given to the printers by actors who transcribed what they remembered from having been in the play, reproducing some parts very accurately and garbling others.

Five early play texts—*Romeo and Juliet* (Q1 1597), *Henry V* (Q1 1600), *The Merry Wives of Windsor* (Q1 1602), *Hamlet* (Q1 1603), and *Pericles* (Q1 1609)—are all suspiciously brief in comparison with subsequent versions, and all five were rejected by John Heminge and Henry Condell when they prepared the First Folio for publication in 1623. In their address to the readers, they rail against "the frauds and stealthes of injurious impostors" who have deceived the book-buying public with "stolne, and surreptitious copies." The Huntington has copies of all five early quartos.

So-called good quartos do not have features suggesting high levels of corruption, but they are not identical to the version of the play printed in the First Folio. So, of the eighteen of Shakespeare's plays that were published before his death, some are "very good," some "very bad," and some are in a quarto form that seems to fall in between. Some quarto texts such as *Richard III* (Q1 1597) and *King Lear* (Q1 1608) are sometimes classified as "doubtful" because they are verbally closer to their counterparts in the

First Folio than those in the "bad" category. However, all these early editions, whether good or bad, are employed by scholars in the arena of literary criticism known as textual studies.

    The most authoritative solution would seem to be to compare the different editions with Shakespeare's own manuscript. But although the British Library does own part of a theatrical manuscript of *The Booke of Sir Thomas More*, in which three leaves of revision are widely thought to be in Shakespeare's handwriting, there are no known copies of any of Shakespeare's plays or his poems in his own hand. Moreover, it is unlikely that Shakespeare took part in the printing of any of his plays and, so far as we know, did not retain a manuscript of any one of them. The only works that Shakespeare published deliberately seem to be *Venus and Adonis* and *The Rape of Lucrece*. Hence the earliest printed editions of *Hamlet* and the other plays (and poems) remain the fundamental sources of our knowledge of Shakespeare. Consequently, a modern edition of a Shakespeare play is often the result of a great deal of scholarly research in the various quarto and folio editions, aimed at creating a text that most closely resembles what Shakespeare might have intended. Despite such scholarship, however, there is no such thing as a "final" version of any of the plays, and this open-endedness is one of the most interesting as well as one of the most frustrating aspects of studying Shakespeare.

TOP: *King Lear*. This painting depicts Lear's reunion with his faithful daughter, Cordelia, who forgives him for banishing her. (4.7)

OVERLEAF: *Hamlet* Q1 (LEFT) and Q2. The first and second quartos of *Hamlet* and the First Folio are crucial to deciding which version Shakespeare actually intended; the Huntington is the only place in the world that has all three.

The Tragedy of Hamlet

And so by continuance, and weakenesse of the braine
Into this frensie, which now possesseth him:
And if this be not true, take this from this.
  King Thinke you t'is so?
  Cor. How? so my Lord, I would very faine know
That thing that I haue saide t'is so, positiuely,
And it hath fallen out otherwise.
Nay, if circumstances leade me on,
Ile finde it out, if it were hid
As deepe as the centre of the earth.
  King. how should wee trie this same?
  Cor. Mary my good lord thus,
The Princes walke is here in the galery,
There let *Ofelia*, walke vntill hee comes:
Your selfe and I will stand close in the study,
There shall you heare the effect of all his hart,
And if it proue any otherwise then loue,
Then let my censure faile an other time.
  King. see where hee comes poring vppon a booke.

Enter Hamlet.

  Cor. Madame, will it please your grace
To leaue vs here?
  Que. With all my hart.   *exit.*
  Cor. And here *Ofelia*, reade you on this booke,
And walke aloofe, the King shal be vnseene.
  Ham. To be, or not to be, I there's the point,
To Die, to sleepe, is that all? I all:
No, to sleepe, to dreame, I mary there it goes,
For in that dreame of death, when wee awake,
And borne before an euerlasting Iudge,
From whence no passenger euer retur'nd,
The vndiscouered country, at whose sight
The happy smile, and the accursed damn'd.
But for this, the ioyfull hope of this,
Whol'd beare the scornes and flattery of the world,
Scorned by the right rich, the rich curssed of the poore?
                                                    The

Prince of Denmarke.

We will bestow our selues; reade on this booke,
That show of such an exercise may cullour
Your lowlines; we are oft too blame in this,
Tis too much proou'd, that with deuotions visage
And pious action, we doe sugar ore
The deuill himselfe.

   King. O tis too true,
How smart a lash that speech doth giue my conscience.
The harlots cheeke beautied with plastring art,
Is not more ougly to the thing that helps it,
Then is my deede to my most painted word :
O heauy burthen.

Enter Hamlet.

   Pol. I heare him comming, with-draw my Lord.
   Ham. To be, or not to be, that is the question,
Whether tis nobler in the minde to suffer
The slings and arrowes of outragious fortune,
Or to take Armes against a sea of troubles,
And by opposing, end them, to die to sleepe
No more, and by a sleepe, to say we end
The hart-ake, and the thousand naturall shocks
That flesh is heire to; tis a consumation
Deuoutly to be wisht to die to sleepe,
To sleepe, perchance to dreame, I there's the rub,
For in that sleepe of death what dreames may come
When we haue shuffled off this mortall coyle
Must giue vs pause, there's the respect
That makes calamitie of so long life :
For who would beare the whips and scornes of time,
Th'oppressors wrong, the proude mans contumely,
The pangs of despiz'd loue, the lawes delay,
The insolence of office, and the spurnes
That patient merrit of th'vnworthy takes,
When he himselfe might his quietas make
With a bare bodkin; who would fardels beare,
To grunt and sweat vnder a wearie life,
But that the dread of something after death,
The vndiscouer'd country, from whose borne

No

As You Like It.
"The fool doth think he
is wise, but the wise man
knows himself to be a
fool." (5.1) Touchstone
the clown shows off for
Audrey in front of her
former suitor, William.

Shakespeare's Sources

O that I had a title good enough to keep his name company!
—THE MERCHANT OF VENICE (3.1.13–14)

The same "unwilling schoolboys" and girls who don't want to read the plays to begin with are often initially outraged to discover that Shakespeare, in conformity with the custom of his time, usually borrowed the stories for his plays, because this kind of "borrowing" is called plagiarism in their classes. An Elizabethan theater audience was not as attuned to the elements of surprise as it was to the gratification of expectations. Shakespeare certainly operated within his theater company in a collaborative manner, and the manner in which he "collaborates" with his sources is interesting and opens up all kinds of profound questions. Shakespeare had a fine eye for a good tale with possibilities of human drama, but if plots were most important we would remember Thomas Lodge, the author of the prose romance *Rosalynde* from whom Shakespeare "borrowed" the plot of *As You Like It*, as readily as we remember Shakespeare. However, we would miss the comic characters of Touchstone, Audrey, William, and Jaques because they are Shakespeare's additions and they serve to turn Lodge's romance into something more satiric. *As You Like It* was published for the first time in the First Folio. Huntington acquired a 1596 copy of *Rosalynde* in 1919.

Similarly, Shakespeare borrowed the plot of *Romeo and Juliet*, and he summarizes it in the prologue to the play. Shakespeare's plot closely follows Arthur Brooke's poem *The Tragicall History of Romeus and Juliet*, which was based on an English stage version of a tale in the famous Italian novella of Matteo Bandello. Brooke, who had seen the stage version, was sufficiently impressed to turn it into a poem. The Huntington Library owns a unique copy of the second edition (1567) of Brooke's poem. Shakespeare read Brooke's version and made a tragic play out of it. Brooke followed the normal Elizabethan practice of pointing to a moral in the story. Shakespeare, however, not only changed the bad poetry into good poetry, but also made the story a tragedy of haste and ill-timing and of passionate young love set in a world—Verona—marred by the passion of adult hate and feuding. *Romeo and Juliet* is often considered the first play in which Shakespeare consistently exhibited his powers of characterization, as stock figures give way to memorable individuals. Because the play was such a huge success, the way was paved for the later achievements of *Hamlet* and *King Lear*.

Queen Elizabeth I. Shakespeare and his acting company depended on the queen's good graces; to please her made good political and financial sense.

The motif of the rope ladder in *The Two Gentlemen of Verona* may also have come from Brooke's *Romeus and Juliet*, while other motifs in the play are found in stories from Boccaccio, Cinthio, and Bandello. A comparison of any of Shakespeare's plays with his sources gives insight into his creative process and his artistry.

Shakespeare's main source for the English history plays was *The Chronicles of England, Scotlande, and Irelande* by the principal historian of Shakespeare's day, Raphael Holinshed. Holinshed first published his chronicles in 1577, so they were fresh and new for Shakespeare's perusal.

Shakespeare probably read the second edition, published in 1587. The Huntington owns five copies of this second edition. *Cymbeline*, another play that owes a debt in terms of incidents and names to Holinshed, appears as the last of the tragedies in the First Folio, although it is really a tragicomedy.

When Queen Elizabeth I died childless on March 24, 1603, the throne went to James VI of Scotland (son of her first cousin Mary, Queen of Scots), who then became James I of England. *Macbeth* was originally printed in the First Folio, but it was written in 1605 or 1606 to commemorate the visit of Christian IV of Denmark to his brother-in-law James I. Shakespeare wrote this play in honor of James, who was reputed to be a descendant of Banquo's line of Scottish kings as recounted in Holinshed's *Chronicles*. The historical Macbeth was a contemporary of Edward the Confessor, king of England from 1042 to 1066; but Shakespeare is much more concerned with the creation of a memorable character than with historical accuracy. There is a superstition that the play is unlucky, and actors will often refer to it as "the Scottish play" instead of by name.

LEFT: Holinshed's *Chronicles* (1587) was a source for at least thirteen of Shakespeare's history plays.

RIGHT: This rare portrait of James I on horseback was executed about the time of Shakespeare's death.

LEFT: *Coriolanus*. The setting is ancient Rome. Menenius has led Coriolanus to the capitol to be invested with the robes of office. (2.3)

RIGHT: *All's Well That Ends Well*. Bertram, two French lords, and some soldiers trick Parolles into revealing his duplicity with a game of "blind man's bluff." (4.3)

Shakespeare's favorite source for the Roman plays was Plutarch's *Lives*, translated into English by Sir Thomas North. The 1579 first edition came to the Huntington in the Bridgewater library purchase. *Julius Caesar*, *Antony and Cleopatra*, and *Timon of Athens* all owe a debt to Plutarch. *Coriolanus* is derived in part from William Camden's *Remaines of a Greater Worke concerning Britaine* (1605). Another important source for romance, comedy, and melodrama is the first translation into English of stories from Boccaccio, Bandello, and other Italian novelists. Compiled and translated by William Painter and called *The Palace of Pleasure*, the work contains the story of Giletta of Narbona, a source for *All's Well That Ends Well*.

Shakespeare based his great tragedy *Othello* on a short story concerning Desdemona and a Moorish captain contained in Giambattista Giraldi's collection entitled *Gli hecatommithi* (The Hundred Tales) and published in Ferrara in 1565. This work did not appear in English in Shakespeare's lifetime, but the French translation of 1583 would have been available to him. Volume I of the two-volume Italian edition is part of the Huntington collection. Again, Shakespeare makes many improvements on the original story, giving us in the "noble" Moor, the most sympathetic of all his tragic heroes. Giraldi's Othello, on the other hand, teams up with Iago to kill Desdemona with a stocking filled with sand. Giraldi, whose academic name was Cynthius (or in Italian, Cinthio), was also a source for two of

Shakespeare's comedies, *All's Well That Ends Well* and *Measure for Measure*, although his proximal source for the latter was probably George Whetstone's play *Promos and Cassandra*.

The Winter's Tale is one of the plays that appeared for the first time in the First Folio of 1623, but its source, the prose romance *Pandosto the Triumph of Time* by Robert Greene, was published in 1595. Huntington acquired a scarce edition of *Pandosto* through the sale in 1919 of part of Christie-Miller's Britwell library. It was Greene who, years before, attacked Shakespeare as "an upstart crow, beautified with our feathers." Once again, we have a chance to see how Shakespeare's imagination worked by comparing his achievement with his source. In Greene's work, Pandosto's wife really dies and is not brought back to life; the old king, not recognizing his daughter, tries to seduce and threatens to rape her—wholly unlike the conclusion of *The Winter's Tale*.

The Winter's Tale. A shepherd and his son discover the baby Perdita on the "shores" of Bohemia. (3.3) Ben Jonson ridiculed Shakespeare's decision to place a shipwreck in landlocked Bohemia.

Antony and Cleopatra. Cleopatra commits suicide with the help of a poisonous snake. (5.2)

The first known printed version of *Anthony and Cleopatra* is that found in the First Folio of 1623, and the play was not published separately until the eighteenth century. The first reference to the play was on May 20, 1608, when Edward Blount entered two items in the Stationers' Register, "A booke called the Booke of Pericles prynce of Tyre" and "A booke called Antony and Cleopatra," thus establishing that both plays existed by then.

A particularly vivid example of Shakespeare's genius in the assimilation and adaptation of source material appears in *Antony and Cleopatra*. For actual passages as well as plot in this play Shakespeare once again drew

freely from North's translation of Plutarch's *Lives*, just as he had done for *Julius Caesar*. In fact *Antony and Cleopatra* picks up almost where *Julius Caesar* left off.

Here is a passage in modernized spelling from North's translation of Plutarch's *Lives* that Shakespeare used as background for describing Cleopatra:

> [Cleopatra would] take her barge in the river of Cydnus, the poop whereof was of gold, the sails of purple, the oars of silver, which kept stroke in rowing after the sound of the music of flutes, hautboys, citherns, viols, and such other instruments as they played upon the barge. And now for the person of her self: she was laid under a pavilion of cloth of gold of tissue, apparelled and attired like the goddess Venus, commonly drawn in picture; and hard by her, on either hand of her pretty fair boys apparelled as painters do set forth god Cupid, with little fans in their hands, with the which they fanned wind upon her. Her ladies and gentlewomen also, the fairest of them were apparelled like the nymphs.

And here is what Shakespeare wrote:

> *The barge she sat in, like a burnish'd throne,*
> *Burnt on the water. The poop was beaten gold,*
> *Purple the sails, and so perfumed that*
> *The winds were love-sick with them; the oars were silver,*
> *Which to the tune of flutes kept stroke, and made*
> *The water which they beat to follow faster,*
> *As amorous of their strokes. For her own person,*
> *It beggar'd all description: she did lie*
> *In her pavilion—cloth of gold, of tissue—*
> *O'er-picturing that Venus where we see*
> *The fancy outwork nature. On each side her*
> *Stood pretty dimpled boys, like smiling Cupids,*
> *With divers-color'd fans, whose wind did seem*
> *To glow the delicate cheeks which they did cool,*
> *And what they undid did.* (2.2.191–205)

When the two are compared, the "original" becomes a foil for the spectacular poetry achieved by Shakespeare.

Tempest

The First Folio, 1623

*The truth is, that the first is equivalent to all others,
and that the rest only deviate from it by the printer's
negligence.... I collated them all at the beginning,
but afterwards used only the first.*

—SAMUEL JOHNSON,
PLAYS OF WILLIAM SHAKESPEARE (1765)

S even years after Shakespeare's death, John Heminge and Henry Condell published the First Folio: *Mr. William Shakespeares Comedies, Histories, & Tragedies. Published according to the True Originall Copies.* One of the Huntington Library's four copies is almost always on display. This first edition of Shakespeare's collected plays includes eighteen that appear in print for the first time, among them *The Taming of the Shrew, Julius Caesar, As You Like It, Twelfth Night, Macbeth, The Tempest,* and *Antony and Cleopatra.*[8]

Book historians disagree on the number of copies published in this edition, with 1,200 as the high estimate and 750 as the low one. Regardless of how many were published, only some 230 to 240 are extant, including "copies" made up from fragments—defective copies were sometimes mined for replacement leaves for more complete copies.[9]

In the First Folio, the address "To the great Variety of Readers" and the dedication to the earl of Pembroke and his brother the earl of Montgomery are signed by John Heminge and Henry Condell, "without ambition either or selfe-profit, or fame: onely to keepe the memory of so worthy a Friend, & Fellow alive, as was our SHAKESPEARE."

The volume also lists "The Names of the Principall Actors in all these Playes," beginning with William Shakespeare and Richard Burbage, and including Heminge and Condell. Condell died in 1627, four years after the publication of the First Folio. That same year Heminge was the active head of the company of actors at the Red Bull who produced some of Shakespeare's plays. The following year, in spite of his age, he was still serving in the difficult and responsible position of paymaster. Heminge died in 1630, two years before the second collected edition of Shakespeare's plays was published.

The famous engraving that appears on the title page of the First Folio (p. 8) is the only known likeness of Shakespeare approved by those who knew him.

OPPOSITE: *The Tempest* appeared in print for the first time in the First Folio. After giving his blessing to Ferdinand and Miranda, Prospero asks Ariel to organize a wedding masque. (4.1)

The Second, Third, & Fourth Folios

More matter with less art.—HAMLET (2.2.95)

The First Folio was a financial success, and the second edition of Shakespeare's collected plays was published in 1632 to meet consumer demand. John Heminge, the editor of the First Folio, had died two years earlier, but his authority as an editor was unquestioned, and the second folio contains the same thirty-six plays as the first. The only difference is the addition of three new commendatory poems, one of them written by a promising young student at Cambridge named John Milton:

An Epitaph on the admirable Dramaticke Poet, W. Shakespeare.

What neede my Shakespeare for his honour'd bones,
The labour of an Age, in piled stones
Or that his hallow'd Reliques should be hid
Under a starre-ypointing [sic] *Pyramid?*
Deare Sonne of Memory, great Heire of Fame,
What needst thou such dull witnesse of thy Name?
Thou in our wonder and astonishment
Hast built thy selfe a lasting Monument:
For whil'st to th'shame of slow-endeavouring Art
Thy easie numbers flow, and that each part,
Hath from the leaves of thy unvalued Booke.
Those Delphicke Lines with deepe Impression tooke
Then thou our fancy of her selfe bereaving,
Dost make us Marble with too much conceiving,
And so Sepulcher'd in such pompe dost lie
That Kings for such a Tombe would wish to die.

Milton wrote this tribute in 1630, five years into the reign of James' son Charles I. During the English Civil Wars, the theaters were closed. Charles I was executed and his love of plays was cited as evidence of his depravity. In 1660 the Stuart monarchy was "restored" in the person of Charles II. Restoration theater had little in common with the Elizabethan, and few of Shakespeare's plays were produced in their original form. Nevertheless, the third folio of Shakespeare's plays was published in 1664. This was believed to be such an improvement over its predecessors that the Bodleian Library disposed of its copy of the First Folio and bought the new edition of 1664 instead. In 1905, the Bodleian was able to identify and buy back its original Folio, but the library was not initially alone in thinking of the First Folio as "outdated." The third and the fourth (1685) folios include seven additional plays, but only *Pericles* is still attributed to Shakespeare. Interestingly, at least one major Restoration playwright, William Congreve, included a First Folio in his private collection.

OPPOSITE: Macbeth and the three witches. "All hail, Macbeth, thou shalt be king hereafter." (1.3)

The Quartos

That book in many's eyes doth share the glory,
That in gold clasps locks in the golden story;
So shall you share all that he doth possess,
By having him, making yourself no less.
          —ROMEO AND JULIET (1.3.91–94)

*A*mong the most precious of the works in the Huntington vault are the rare, early editions of the quartos. The collection includes the first and second quartos of *Romeo and Juliet* (1597 and 1599) and of *Hamlet* (1603 and 1604). In fact, the Huntington is the only library to possess both of the *Hamlet* quartos. The collection also includes the first quartos of *Richard III* (1597), *The Merry Wives of Windsor* (1602), *A Midsummer Night's Dream* (1600), and *Love's Labor's Lost* (1598).

OPPOSITE:
"O Romeo, Romeo! Wherefore art thou Romeo? Deny thy father and refuse thy name…"

LEFT: *The Two Gentlemen of Verona*. Launce (originally played by Will Kempe) says, "I think Crab, my dog be the sourest dog that lives." (2.3)

RIGHT: *A Midsummer Night's Dream*. Oberon sends the knavish Puck to fetch a white-and-purple flower called "love in idleness." (2.1)

Much Ado About Nothing.

TOP: Dogberry (RIGHT) and Verges, the lawmen, enter with the watch. (3.3)

BOTTOM: Hero and Ursula have plotted to have Beatrice overhear them talk about Benedict. (3.1)

COMEDIES

A first quarto edition of *A Pleasant Conceited Comedie called, Loves Labors lost. As it was presented before her Highnes this last Christmas* was published in 1598. Despite the phrase on the title page "Newly corrected and augmented By W. Shakespere," no earlier version is known to exist. *Love's Labor's Lost* is one of the few Shakespeare plays for which no definite source is known and is an unusual comedy because no one gets married, as happens in all of his other comedies.

Two years later (1600) the first quarto of *A Midsommer nights dreame. As it hath beene sundry times publickely acted, by the Right honourable, the Lord Chamberlaine his servants* was published, drawing from sources as diversified as Geoffrey Chaucer, the Roman poet Ovid, North's translation of Plutarch's *Lives*, native fairy lore, and Shakespeare's own knowledge of amateur theatricals. From performance records, we know the play was written about 1595 and may well have been commissioned for an important wedding.

A Most pleasaunt and excellent conceited Comedie, of Syr John Falstaffe, and the merrie Wives of Windsor appeared in quarto in 1602. The first edition is a badly garbled version, only half as long as the text in the First Folio. Tradition has it that the play was written in less than two weeks by special command of Queen Elizabeth for a royal performance at Windsor. The title page does say that the play had often been acted "before Her Majestie, and else-where."

Paying $10,000, Mr. Huntington acquired a perfect copy of the first edition of *Much Ado About Nothing* (1600) in 1918. The play would have been first staged in 1589 or 1590 with Will Kempe, famous for his preposterous antics as Dogberry, the constable. The Hero-Claudio subplot of a young woman falsely slandered derives from two Italian sources: a traditional story told by Ariosto in *Orlando Furioso* and another version by Matteo Bandello.

The Huntington also owns two copies of *The most excellent Historie of the Merchant of Venice* (1600)—a disturbing play. It is classified as a comedy and ends with general joy, but often seems to be more about hate than love, with Shylock's bloodthirsty demand for a "pound of flesh." Modern discussions of the play generally center on Shylock and Shakespeare's attitude toward Jews, who were expelled from England by Edward I in 1290. Launcelot Gobbo, the clown, is a type well known in Italian *commèdia*, where he was probably played as a hunchback or dwarf. Two popular sayings come to us from the play's text: "mine own flesh and blood" (2.2.92) and "All that glisters is not gold" (2.7.65).

OVERLEAF

LEFT: *Love's Labor's Lost.* Costard flirts with Jaquenetta (4.3). This play is as much about language as it is about love and contains the longest word in the Shakespeare canon, "honorificabilitudinitatibus," defined as "the condition of being burdened with multiple honors."

RIGHT: In *The Merchant of Venice*, Antonio borrows money from Shylock, promising to forfeit "a pound of flesh" if he can't make good on the loan. (1.3)

In the First Folio, *The Tragedie of Troylus and Cressida* appears to be an addition between *Henry VIII*, a history, and *Coriolanus*, a tragedy, but it is not listed in the table of contents. More recently it has been lumped together with *All's Well That Ends Well* and *Measure for Measure* as another "problem play," because it resists classification as either a comedy or tragedy. All three "problem" plays might better be described as black comedies or satires. The Huntington owns a first quarto (first state) of 1609, titled *The Famous Historie of Troylus and Cresseid*. The story of Cressida's betrayal came from Chaucer's poem *Troilus and Criseyde* and was well known to Elizabethans.

The Huntington also has a first quarto of *The late, And much admired Play, called Pericles, Prince of Tyre* printed in 1609. For reasons unknown, *Pericles* was not among the plays included in the First Folio of 1623. The play was entered in the Stationers' Register in 1608, but was not published until 1609, when Henry Gosson printed two quarto editions. Many scholars feel that the first two acts reflect work primarily by an unknown collaborator, and Ben Jonson declared it a "mouldy tale."[10] The distancing choruses are presented by a character representing John Gower, who wrote the poem *Confessio Amantis*, a source for *Pericles*. There is a marked difference

Troilus and Cressida. Title page of the first quarto (first state) of 1609.

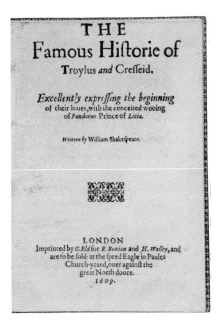

THE
Famous Historie of
Troylus *and* Cresseid.

Excellently expressing the beginning
of their loues, with the conceited wooing
of *Pandarus* Prince of *Licia.*

Written by William Shakespeare.

LONDON
Imprinted by *G. Eld* for *R. Bonian* and *H. Walley*, and
are to be sold at the spred Eagle in Paules
Church-yeard, ouer against the
great North doore.
1609.

between the choruses prefixed to the first two acts and the choruses of the later, or Shakespearean part, which are more like the choruses in *Henry V*. The text of the 1609 quarto seems to have been reconstructed from memory by actors. *Pericles* is the first of the reconciliation "romances" that mark Shakespeare's great final phase as a dramatic writer, and the play is particularly known for the brothel scenes, which juxtapose virtue and vice. The theme of patience under adversity is common in his later works. The "Patient Pericles" is noticeably different from Apollonius, his counterpart in Gower.

Pericles is the only one of Shakespeare's plays omitted from the 1623 Folio. At Mytilene, Marina has been sold to a brothel run by Bawd and her servant Boult. (4.2)

The Two Noble Kinsmen: Presented at the Blackfriers by the Kings Maiesties servants, with great applause: Written by the memorable Worthies of their time. Mr. John Fletcher, and Mr. William Shakespeare. Gent was a collaboration between Shakespeare and John Fletcher. Fletcher, a younger colleague who was to succeed Shakespeare as chief dramatist for the King's Men, was the primary author. Shakespeare probably worked on the first and last acts. The "noble" kinsmen are brothers who have a falling out because they both love Emilian, the sister of Hippolyta from *A Midsummer Night's Dream*. In fact both plays begin with the wedding of Theseus and Hippolyta. None of the four folio editions includes a copy of this play, and it has only recently been added to collected editions of Shakespeare's works. The Huntington has a copy of the original quarto edition printed by Thomas Cotes in 1634.

HISTORIES

In his history plays, Shakespeare explored the bloody power struggles that preceded the Tudors. The first tetralogy, *Henry VI, Parts 1, 2, and 3* and *Richard III*, covers the period from 1422 to 1485, during the War of the Roses between the families of Lancaster and York. The first edition of *Richard III* was followed by seven more quarto versions printed over the next forty years. The Huntington's first edition of *The Tragedy of King Richard the third* was published in quarto form in 1597, apparently from a prompter's copy, and is therefore probably authentic. The play is founded chiefly on historical accounts from Holinshed's *Chronicles* and Edward Hall's *Union of the two noble and illustre famelies of Lancastre & Yorke*. *Richard III* was probably performed as early as 1592. It no doubt owed its immediate and long-continued popularity to the portrayal of Richard by the leading actor of the Lord Chamberlain's Men, Richard Burbage, for whom Shakespeare wrote many of his great tragic parts, including Hamlet and King Lear. Some critics think of Richard as Shakespeare's first really memorable character. The second quartos of *Richard II* and *Richard III*, both published in 1598, are the first of Shakespeare's works to have his name on the title page.

Richard III and *The First Part of King Henry IV* were the most popular of the history plays, and each had been published in six quarto editions before appearing in the First Folio. The Huntington owns a second quarto edition of *The History of Henrie the Fourth; with the battell at Shrewsburie,*

Richard III begins where *Henry VI, Part 3* leaves off. The myth of the murderous hunchbacked king owes more to rumor and Tudor propaganda than to historical fact.

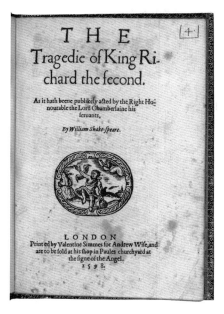

LEFT: Richard Burbage was the resident tragedian in the Lord Chamberlain's acting company. Shakespeare wrote some of his greatest roles for the actor, including Richard III, Hamlet, and King Lear.

RIGHT: *Richard II*, title page of second quarto (1598). This history play has been called a tragedy because it depicts the character of Richard as a man as well as a king.

dated 1598,[11] and another edition from 1599 with "Newly corrected by W. Shake-speare" added to the title, although there is no evidence that Shakespeare was involved with its publication.

Richard II, *Henry IV Parts 1 and 2*, and *Henry V* make up the second tetralogy of history plays. They take a look at an earlier period in history leading up to the Wars of the Roses. Each history play addresses the theme of effective leadership. The Huntington owns a 1597 edition of *The tragedie of king Richard the second*. Two more editions followed in 1598. The collection also includes a quarto of *Henry V* dated 1600.

Globe Theater. *King Henry V* was probably the first play to grace the stage of this theater, which opened in 1599.

The first performance of *King Henry IV, Part 2*, took place about 1597. The play was subsequently published in 1600 under the title *The Second part of Henrie the fourth, continuing to his death, and coronation of Henrie the fift. With the humours of sir John Falstaffe, and swaggering Pistoll.* Part 2 picks up where Part 1 left off, with rumors that Prince Hal has died and that Hotspur and his Scottish ally Douglas have defeated King Henry IV. There were two variants published in 1600. In the second, two leaves are replaced with four leaves containing a new scene. Both variants are in the Huntington collection. Falstaff first appeared in *King Henry IV, Part 1*, which was published in 1598; these plays made him one of the most popular characters in theatrical history. His girth is the subject of much humor, as is his penchant for drinking and women.

Shakespeare pursues his exploration of the theories of kingship in two other history plays, *King John* and *Henry VIII*, both of which fall outside the time span of the two tetralogies. The Huntington owns a 1611 quarto of *King John*. Although this play is seldom performed, it is ironically the subject of the first movie ever made of a Shakespeare play: a four-minute film version made by Sir Herbert Beerbohm Tree in London in 1899.

Even though John Fletcher was the primary author of *Henry VIII*, the play appears in the First Folio without reference to Fletcher, who also collaborated with Shakespeare on the lost play *Cardenio*. *Henry VIII* ends with the birth of Princess Elizabeth who, of course, became Elizabeth I. It was during a performance of *King Henry VIII* in 1613 that the Globe Theater's thatch roof caught fire and the playhouse burned down.

Shakespeare has finally begun to be accepted as the author of at least part of *Edward III*. As early as 1760, Cambridge scholar Edward Capell made a claim for including *Edward III* in the canon, but only recently have most scholars come to agreement that Shakespeare contributed to the first two acts. The Huntington owns quartos from 1596 and 1599 of *The Raigne of King Edward the third: As it hath bin sundrie times plaied about the Citie of London.* In 1997 *Edward III* was included in the revised second edition of the *Riverside Shakespeare*, and in 1999 members of the Royal Shakespeare Company gave it a public reading in Stratford-on-Avon.

Titus Andronicus. In Rome, Titus pleads to the Tribunes to let his sons live, but they ignore him. (3.1)

Julius Caesar. The ghost of Caesar enters Brutus's tent. (4.3)

TRAGEDIES

Shakespeare's tragedies bring together the dramatic traditions of the classical and the medieval. *Othello*, *Hamlet*, *Macbeth*, and *King Lear* are often referred to as Shakespeare's great tragedies, but each of his tragedies encompasses one or more of life's fundamental problems and the struggles of men and women to resolve them.

The revenge tragedy *Titus Andronicus* is the first of Shakespeare's plays to appear in print, and it is his most gruesome achievement. Everything else he wrote seems refined in contrast to this, his first tragedy, packed with mutilations and references to animals, hunting, and revenge. Titus sacrifices his enemy's eldest son by hacking off his limbs and throwing him into a fire. Titus's daughter is raped, her tongue and hands amputated, and her husband decapitated. Titus loses a hand and his sons lose their heads. He retaliates by tricking his nemesis into dining unwittingly on her murdered children. The play is what some might call "gross." Jonson made fun of it in the "Induction" to his play *Bartholomew Fair* (1614). It is interesting to compare Titus with Shakespeare's later tragic heroes, especially Othello and Lear, as well as with the play's obvious sources and inspirations, including the works of Kyd, Marlowe, Ovid, Seneca, and the Roman historians.

According to Philip Henslowe's diary, *Titus Andronicus* was produced in 1594. Three quarto editions of the play appeared before it was published in the First Folio. The Huntington owns quartos from 1600 and 1611. Act 2, scene 2 appears only in the First Folio. The sole surviving copy of *Titus Andronicus* from 1594 was discovered in Sweden in 1904 and is owned by the Folger. Since this discovery, modern editions of *Titus* omit the last four lines as they were printed in the First Folio. Textual analysis has determined the Folio text was prepared from the third quarto, a reprint of the second, and the final lines about Aaron's villainy appear to have been composed by a printer.

For many years *Julius Caesar* was the Shakespeare play most often read in American high schools. As early as 1895 it was included in the first English literature curriculum for a New York City high school. *Julius Caesar* remains a popular choice for young students because it is an excellent tool for teaching rhetoric and speech and has none of the sexual double-entendres common in many of Shakespeare's other plays. Shakespeare derived the great body of his historical material from North's translation of Plutarch's *Lives*, first printed in 1579 and dedicated to Queen Elizabeth.

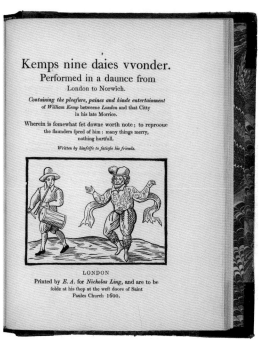

LEFT: *Romeo and Juliet.* Romeo tries to get a word with Juliet's nurse in this group that includes Mercutio, Benvolio, and Peter. (2.4)

RIGHT: This illustration appeared on a pamphlet celebrating Kempe's "nine daies wonder," during which he danced from London to Norwich in 1600.

We learn a great deal about Shakespeare the writer from analyzing the ways in which he amplifies some of his source material, while simplifying and compressing some of the action for dramatic effect. The play was first printed, so far as we know, in the First Folio. The Huntington owns a copy of the earliest known quarto, titled *Julius Caesar. A tragedy. As it is now acted at the Theatre Royal* (1684).

The Huntington has first and second quartos of *An Excellent conceited Tragedie of Romeo and Juliet,* neither of which bears Shakespeare's name on the title page. The 1597 first quarto was printed from a short and somewhat corrupt text. It differs from the 1599 second quarto, which may belong to an older version of the play almost certainly printed from Shakespeare's own handwritten copy. One indication of this is a stage direction giving the name of the actor Will Kempe rather than of the character Peter. The best comedic role in the play is that of the Nurse. Peter, her servant, has very few lines. Kempe was probably the most popular "clown" of the period, and he certainly helped to establish the early success of the Lord Chamberlain's Men. Although the company did not use the star system, Kempe's popularity as an actor perhaps led Shakespeare to write a small part for him in this play, and it is an interesting insight into the way the company functioned, since they evidently felt that Kempe could be used to advantage in a small role. In any case, the clown parts as printed were only springboards for improvisation on the stage. The Globe was the first playhouse to be partly owned by the actors, including both Kempe and Shakespeare, although Kempe sold his share and left the company in 1599.

The story of Hamlet was an ancient one, as contemporary allusions show, and it had already been made into a popular revenge play, perhaps by Thomas Kyd. In his *Hamlet* Shakespeare made use both of that play and certain early narrative versions of the story available to him. There is no doubt that Richard Burbage was the first Shakespearean Hamlet, and the part, after almost 400 years, continues to be the goal of many serious actors.

The first quarto edition of *The Tragicall Historie of Hamlet Prince of Denmarke* was printed in 1603 by Valentine Simmes for Nicholas Ling and John Trundell. In 1604 the second quarto of *Hamlet*, longer by 2,200 lines, was published. There are only two known copies of the first quarto. Neither is complete. That in the British Library lacks the title page, whereas the Huntington Library copy is without the last leaf. The Huntington is the only library having both the first and second quartos, which makes the library an important resource for scholars engaged in textual criticism. Both were purchased by Mr. Huntington in 1914 as part of the Kemble-Devonshire collection. In 1918 he added the third edition of *Hamlet* (1611) to his holdings.

In Hamlet's rambling, illogical, melodramatic first soliloquy, he expresses his despair. Here is the beginning of the passage in the form we usually hear or read it:

> *O that this too too sallied flesh would melt,*
> *Thaw, and resolve itself into a dew!*
> *Or that the Everlasting had not fix'd*
> *His canon 'gainst self-slaughter! O God, God,*
> *How weary, stale, flat, and unprofitable*
> *Seem to me all the uses of this world!* (1.2.129–34)

In the first quarto of 1603 the words are:

> *O that this too much griev'd and sallied flesh*
> *Would melt to nothing, or that the universall*
> *Globe of heaven would turne al to a Chaos!*

In the second quarto (1604), instead of regretting the law against "self-slaughter," he laments "seale slaughter" and instead of "the uses of the world" being "weary", they are "wary."

Artist's interpretation of Hamlet's visit to Ophelia as she describes it to her father. (2.1)

In the best-known passage from the play (see pp. 20–21), Hamlet says, as we usually remember it:

To be, or not to be, that is the question:
Whether 'tis nobler in the mind to suffer
The slings and arrows of outrageous fortune,
Or to take arms against a sea of troubles,
And by opposing, end them. (3.1.55–59)

But not according to the first quarto, where it is placed earlier in the play and reads:

To be, or not to be, I there's the point,
To Die, to sleepe, is that all? I all:
No, to sleepe, to dreame, I mary there it goes,
For in that dreame of death, when wee awake,
And borne before an everlasting Judge,
From whence no passenger ever retur'nd, …

Why the startling, sometimes laughable, differences, and why are we more familiar with the 1604 version? Until the 1980s, scholars had largely agreed that the first text is a "bad" or unauthorized quarto, reconstructed from memory by one or two of the actors, while Q2 is a revised edition, probably prepared by Shakespeare's acting company. Hence Q2 was heralded on its title page as "Newly imprinted and enlarged to almost as much againe as it was, according to the true and perfect Coppie." Modern criticism resists the phrase "bad quarto" as too pejorative, especially if it is used to mean the text is corrupt or "not authorial." Some quartos may even be earlier drafts of plays providing us with insight into Shakespeare's creative process.

In a letter dated 1771 Thomas Jefferson had occasion to write: "A lively and lasting sense of filial duty is more effectually impressed on the mind of a son or daughter by reading King Lear, than by all the dry volumes of ethics, and divinity that ever were written."[12] There has been a lot of discussion in recent years about the quarto text of *King Lear* and its interesting variations from the First Folio. Indeed, two quarto editions of *Lear* appeared before the First Folio, both dated 1608. Q2 was actually printed in 1619 and falsely dated by an unscrupulous printer who simply reset Q1. The Huntington owns copies of both.

We don't know when *King Lear* was composed or first performed, but the title page of Q1 helps us to date the play's composition as some time before December 1607, for we are told that the text is "As it was played before the Kings Maiestie at Whitehall upon S. Stephans night in Christmas Hollidayes. By his Maiesties servants playing usually at the Gloabe on the Bancke-side." And, since it appears clear that Shakespeare had a close knowledge of a play published anonymously in 1605 as *The True Chronicle History of King Leir, and his three daughters, Gonorill, Ragan, and Cordella*, we can place Shakespeare's composition as not before 1605.

King Lear and his fool.
On the stormy heath,
Lear hurls his defiance at
the elements. (3.2)

Interestingly, when the Folio text of *King Lear* appeared in 1623, it showed major changes, including the addition of about 100 lines and the omission of a whole scene of about 300 lines. Although there is no evidence that Shakespeare made these changes, many scholars argue that it is reasonable to assume he did because they are changes of literary and dramatic merit.

Nahum Tate (1652–1715), an English poet laureate and dramatist, wrote several popular adaptations of Shakespeare, the most famous being his *King Lear*. In his play (published in 1681) Tate omitted the part of the Fool and had Cordelia survive to marry Edgar. Tate wasn't the only writer to give Lear a happier ending. There are more than forty versions of the story, many taken from *King Leir* (ca. 1590), the first dramatic version of the story. The others all allow Cordelia to live "happily ever after."

Othello. Desdemona fell in love with the exotic Moor, Othello, because of the many dangers he had faced. (1.3)

In 1622, six years after Shakespeare's death, a quarto edition of *Othello* appeared that is about 160 lines shorter than the version commonly used today. The second version appeared in the First Folio and is thought by most contemporary editors to be more reliable. Q1 includes a number of oaths that are not in the Folio, and it also has additional stage directions. A second quarto was printed from the Folio in 1630. Most scholars believe the Folio version is "more Shakespearean." As discussed previously, the source for the play is a tale by the Italian writer Cinthio in his *Gli hecatommithi*. In an English translation of 1855, the Cinthio story begins: "There once lived in Venice a Moor, who was very valiant, and of a handsome person; and having given proofs in war of great skill and prudence, he was highly esteemed by the Signoria of the Republic, who in rewarding deeds of valour advanced the interests of the State."

This Shadowe is renowned Shakespear's? Soule of th'age
The applause! delight! the wonder of the Stage.
Nature her selfe, was proud of his designes
And joy'd to weare the dressing of his lines,
The learned will Confess, his works are such,
As neither man, nor Muse, can prayse to much.
For ever live thy fame, the world to tell,
Thy like, no age, shall ever paralell.

W. M. sculpsit.

The Poems

...the first heire of my invention...
—*VENUS AND ADONIS*, DEDICATION

THE GREAT NARRATIVE POEMS

Shakespeare's first published works were the two long narrative poems *Venus and Adonis* and *The Rape of Lucrece*. The stories for these poems come from ancient Greece and Rome. Their popularity in Shakespeare's lifetime is attested to by the fact that *Venus and Adonis* went through ten editions and *Lucrece* three. The first poem is a lusty love story; the second, set well before the time of Julius Caesar, is a tragedy. Both poems were dedicated to Henry Wriothesley, third earl of Southampton, who was a generous patron of Shakespeare and other poets. In his dedication to *Venus and Adonis*, Shakespeare refers to the poem as "the first heire of my invention," suggesting that it was the first poem he deemed worthy of publication, not necessarily the first he had written.

The Huntington holds first editions of *The Rape of Lucrece* (1594), *The Passionate Pilgrime* (1599), and the Sonnets (the two variants of 1609), as well as the only known copy of the fourth edition of *Venus and Adonis* (1599), bound with *The Passionate Pilgrime* (1599) and *Epigrammes and Elegies* by Sir John Davies (1599?).

OPPOSITE: Shakespeare's portrait by William Marshall in *Poems: Written by Wil. Shakespeare. Gent.*, published in 1640.

LEFT: The Honorable Henry Wriothesley, third earl of Southampton, was one candidate for "W.H." in the sonnets' dedication.

If Shakespeare had been a gentleman, the poems would probably not have been published at all, for gentlemen circulated their work only in manuscript and did not permit it to be read by the general public. Shakespeare's choice for printer and publisher was Richard Field, son of Henry Field of Stratford, a neighbor of Shakespeare's father. Field had his own press and was one of the twenty-two master printers permitted to operate in London at the time. In April 1593, Field filed notice with the Company of Stationers that he was the owner of "a booke entituled Venus and Adonis." The only known copy of the first edition of *Venus and Adonis* (1593) is in the Bodleian Library. The Huntington has one of four known copies of the second edition (1594), as well as the only known copy of one of the 1599 editions mentioned above. In 1594 narrative poems were much more lucrative than plays, and it appeared at that time that Shakespeare was much more likely to be remembered for *Venus and Adonis* and *Lucrece* than for any of his dramas.

THE SONNETS

The year 1609 marks the first publication of all 154 of Shakespeare's sonnets by the printer George Eld for the publisher Thomas Thorpe.

Sonnets, comprising fourteen lines of rhymed iambic pentameter, were very much in vogue during the 1590s, especially following the publication of Sir Philip Sidney's sonnet sequence *Astrophel and Stella* in 1591. In fact, 1592–93, when the theaters were closed by the plague, is sometimes seen as the prime sonnet-writing time. Because Shakespeare's sonnets are written in the first person, many readers have wistfully, or maybe wishfully, read them with the desire to discover something about Shakespeare's private life. But while the sonnets are almost certainly rooted in personal experience, to read them as autobiography is probably to be "unlearned in the world's false subtleties" (SONNET 138, LINE 4).

Great poetry is created not only in response to private feelings, but also in response to the times in which it is written, expressing what other people are feeling before they are aware of it themselves. When Shakespeare becomes aware of "himself," bitter, disgusted—these qualities mark his finest sonnets. The self-analysis, the self-conflict, is what keeps us transfixed by his great plays.

In this scene from
Measure for Measure,
Isabella asks for
Justice, O royal duke! (5.1)
Excerpts from this play
appear in *Poems*.

MINOR POEMS AND THE COLLECTED POEMS

In 1599 there appeared in print for the first time *The Passionate Pilgrime. By W. Shakespeare*, a collection of twenty short poems, only five of which are without doubt Shakespeare's. The Huntington copy is bound together with the only known copy of the 1599 edition of *Venus and Adonis*. These two rare treasures came to the Huntington from the old library at Lamport Hall in Northamptonshire.

"The Phoenix and the Turtle," also in the Huntington collection, is an allegorical poem by Shakespeare describing the funeral of two lovers. The turtle is actually a turtledove, a symbol of faithfulness in love, and the phoenix is a mythological bird symbolizing immortality. Shakespeare's poem is printed as part of a supplement of poetical essays to Robert Chester's *Loves Martyr: Or, Rosalin's Complaint* (1601). Though Shakespeare's contribution is untitled, his name is printed at the end of this poem.

The Huntington's *Poems: Written by Wil. Shakespeare. Gent.*, first published in 1640, is one of the rare copies that contain two title pages and the portrait by William Marshall. The content consists of *The Passionate Pilgrim*, "A Lover's Complaint," "The Phoenix and the Turtle," all but eight of the sonnets, some excerpts from *Measure for Measure* and *As You Like It*, as well as poems by miscellaneous authors.

Friends, Foes, Fakes, and Forgeries

O brave new world
That has such people in 't!
—THE TEMPEST (5.1.183–84)

SHAKESPEARE'S LITERARY CONTEMPORARIES

Shakespeare lived from 1564 to 1616. The galaxy of his literary contemporaries is represented in the Huntington collection by a wealth of rare editions. Of the great playwrights, Christopher Marlowe was born in the same year as Shakespeare and died in 1593. The Library's *Tamburlaine the Great* (parts 1 and 2) is the only known complete copy of the first edition of Marlowe's tragedy. The play was performed by the Lord Admiral's Men. It may have been from Marlowe that Shakespeare learned to concentrate on a single imposing figure and to produce masterful blank verse. The great Edward Alleyn, principal actor of the Lord Admiral's Men, played the character of Tamburlaine.

Thomas Kyd (1557–1594) preceded Shakespeare in birth and death. The Huntington copy of Kyd's popular *Spanish Tragedie* is the only one from the 1599 edition now known to exist. Kyd's tragedy, originally published in 1592, was the pattern for subsequent revenge plays and was in this respect a strong influence upon Shakespeare's *Titus Andronicus* and *Hamlet*.

The Huntington's rich collection of works from the Shakespearean age is too vast to enumerate here, but a highlight is the first edition of Sir Philip Sidney's *The Countesse of Pembrokes Arcadia* printed in 1590. This much-loved and widely read book suggested to Shakespeare the tragic Gloucester subplot in *King Lear*. The Library also holds rare early copies of Spenser's *Faerie Queene*.

A first edition of John Lyly's *Endimion, The Man in the Moone*, the drama whose influence shows in Shakespeare's early witty and sophisticated comedies such as *Love's Labor's Lost*, is part of the collection, as is the earliest edition of Thomas Heywood's *The Rape of Lucrece. A True Roman Tragedie*, published in 1608. Shakespeare had treated this famous story in his narrative poem *The Rape of Lucrece* as early as 1594. Ben Jonson wrote many of his plays for Shakespeare's company, but his satiric tragedy *Sejanus His Fall*, written in the wake of the popularity of Shakespeare's *Julius Caesar* (1599), was not successful on the stage. One of the Huntington's copies of the first extant edition (1605) bears a presentation inscription in Ben Jonson's handwriting to his friend Sir Francis Crane.

OPPOSITE: Shakespeare with Ben Jonson at the Mermaid Tavern, a gathering place for writers in London.

LEFT: Ben Jonson was Shakespeare's younger contemporary and principal rival as a playwright.

RIGHT: Thomas Kyd's *The Spanish Tragedie* may have been an influence on Shakespeare's *Hamlet*.

During Shakespeare's lifetime actors and playwrights existed in a collaborative environment. The biographer Nicholas Rowe in his *Works* (1709) has Shakespeare's company give an unknown Jonson his first play commission, but the Rowe biography is unsubstantiated in many respects. We do know that in 1598 Shakespeare acted in Jonson's first play, *Every Man in His Humour,* for the Lord Chamberlain's Men and that Jonson was paid to write scenes for the 1602 revision of Kyd's *Spanish Tragedie.*

In 2000 and 2001, long-time Renaissance scholar and Huntington reader James Riddell donated twenty-five copies of the first folio of Ben Jonson's *Works* (1616) and numerous copies of the later second volume. Added to the Huntington's previous holdings, this brings the Jonson folios to thirty copies total. Not only does this give scholars the opportunity to study the numerous textual variants produced during the printing process, it also lets them compare the physical evidence of the various lives the copies have led since leaving the printing shop.

THE AUTHORSHIP QUESTION

> *I am "a sort of" haunted by the conviction that the*
> *divine William is the biggest and most successful*
> *fraud ever practised on a patient world.*
>
> —HENRY JAMES, 1903[13]

Henry James was not alone in his suspicion that Shakespeare didn't write the plays and poems attributed to him. In the nearly four centuries since Shakespeare's death various people have felt compelled to assert that somebody else actually wrote them. They argue that "Shakespeare's" vocabulary runs to more than twenty-one thousand words, as compared with Milton's eight thousand, and that a man with his modest beginnings is unlikely to have reinvented the English language the way the plays have done. Another illustrious doubter was Sigmund Freud, who wrote in his *Outline of Psychoanalysis* (1940) that "The name 'William Shakespeare' is most probably a pseudonym behind which there lies concealed a great unknown."

While it is likely that other writers penned at least some parts of some of the plays, this is a far cry from the argument that Shakespeare was a country bumpkin who couldn't possibly have written them. Shakespeare's life and activities are recorded in more than a hundred contemporary documents, which ought "to give the world assurance of a man" (*Hamlet* 3.4.62). Among the Huntington's holdings of numerous broadsides on the occasion of the death of Queen Elizabeth in 1603 is *A mournefull Dittie, entituled Elizabeths losse, together with a welcome for King James*, with the challenge:

> *You Poets all brave Shakespeare,*
> *Johnson, Greene,*
> *Bestow your time to write*
> *For Englands Queene.*

The First Folio by itself would be sufficient evidence of the existence and identity of Shakespeare, with its portrait, two corroborating poems by Ben Jonson (whose existence no one doubts), and a full explanation by the two partners who collected these thirty-six plays for publication. A memorial poem in the Folio makes specific reference linking William Shakespeare the playwright to the William Shakespeare of Stratford. Leonard Digges writes:

> *Shake-speare, at length thy pious fellowes give*
> *The world thy Workes: thy Workes, by which, out-live*
> *Thy Tombe, thy name must when that stone is rent*
> *And time dissolves thy Stratford Monument,*
> *Here we alive shall view thee still.*

To Robert Greene (1558–1592), poet, pamphleteer, and first great English master of dramatic plot, Shakespeare was "an upstart Crow, beautified with our feathers, that with his Tygers hart wrapt in a Players hyde, supposes he is as well able to bombast out a blanke verse as the best of you." The allusion appears on page F1v in the pamphlet *Greenes, Groats-worth of Witte*, published the year its author died, and is the first known published reference to Shakespeare as a playwright. Greene was probably reminded of the crow in Aesop's *Fables* who strutted in borrowed feathers. At any rate it is a delightful image of a young Shakespeare, who was just beginning to make a name for himself.

From the wealth of such contemporary materials in the Huntington collection the little book *Palladis Tamia* (1598) by Francis Meres is the most important because it enumerates Shakespeare's plays and makes many references to the poet and his literary contemporaries. It contains the famous commendation, "so the sweete wittie soule of Ovid lives in melliflous & hony-tongued Shakespeare, witnes his Venus and Adonis, his Lucrece, his sugred Sonnets among his private friends, &c." (pp. 281B–282A).

But mysteries are exciting, and one way to keep alive the authorship question over the years was to create evidence by forging it. The two most active practitioners of this art have been William Henry Ireland in the eighteenth century and John Payne Collier in the nineteenth. The Huntington Library has the principal holdings of the works of both Ireland and Collier.

Ireland (1777–1835), youthful son of author and book dealer Samuel Ireland, deceived the literary world (and his father) with a series of remarkable Shakespearean forgeries. His "Shakespearean documents" were published in 1796 as *Miscellaneous Papers and Legal Instruments under the Hand and Seal of William Shakespeare*, edited in good faith by his father. The copy in the Huntington Library belonged to William Henry Ireland himself and is copiously annotated by him and extra-illustrated with the "original" documents concerned. These documents include Ireland's forgery of a letter supposed to have been written by Shakespeare to Anne Hathaway, together with an etching of a purported lock of the poet's hair, as well as a new scene for *King Lear* and a new scene for *Hamlet*. In one of his manuscript letters, Ireland wrote, "My motto is NEMO SINE VITIIS (No one without his faults)"—enough said.

Collier, the nineteenth-century scholar and forger, produced a copy of the second folio of 1632 that was annotated throughout in a hand alleged to be of the early seventeenth century. It is known as the "Perkins

OPPOSITE: Francis Bacon was a prolific writer, but his style was different from Shakespeare's.

Edward de Vere,
seventeenth earl of
Oxford, died in 1604,
before some of
Shakespeare's best plays
were written.

Folio" because of a previous owner's name written on the leather binding. Collier claimed that the annotator of the Perkins Folio had had access to better texts than did those who collected the plays for the First Folio. He announced his discovery in 1852 and began publishing the results, which created an uproar of astonishment; but it was ultimately concluded that Collier himself had made all the changes and additions.

In 1995 the Huntington acquired the Francis Bacon Library, which had been founded by Walter Conrad Arensberg in 1938. Francis Bacon has been the favorite candidate for authorship of those who doubted that Shakespeare wrote the plays and poems attributed to him, and Arensberg was one of the believers in Bacon. Most scholars agree, however, that Bacon was simply too busy a statesman to moonlight as Shakespeare and that his literary style doesn't match the style of Shakespeare's plays and poems. In fact, since the 1920s, the chief contender has been Edward de Vere, seventeenth earl of Oxford. De Vere's fans, known as Oxfordians, contend that he had the money, breeding, and education which "Shakespeare" needed to write sophisticated lyrics grounded in an extraordinary depth and range of learning. The third major "alternative" is Christopher Marlowe, but in all, nearly sixty claimants to the title have been put forward.

PLAYS ATTRIBUTED TO SHAKESPEARE

Not only has Shakespeare been accused of fraud, he has also been given credit for plays he almost certainly did not write. As his name and his plays became well known, London printers and publishers decided to cash in on his popularity and began issuing plays by other writers and

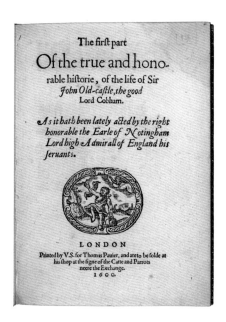

The first part

Of the true and hono-

rable hiſtorie, of the life of Sir
John Old-caſtle, the good
Lord Cobham.

*As it hath been lately acted by the right
honorable the Earle of Notingham
Lord high Admirall of England his
Seruants.*

LONDON

Printed by V.S. for Thomas Pauier, and are to be ſolde at
his ſhop at the ſigne of the Catte and Parrots
neere the Exchange.
1 6 0 0.

announcing that they were written by Shakespeare. First editions of four such plays are part of the Huntington collection: *The Lamentable and True Tragedie of M. Arden of Feversham in Kent*, first published in 1592, is the earliest of the four. The plot of the play derives from a striking sex murder in the town of Feversham; somebody, but not Shakespeare, made the grisly episode into a popular play.

A Most Pleasant Comedie of Mucedorus, published in 1598, was a reliable old comedy of Shakespeare's era. Certain "new additions" referred to in a later edition are superior to the rest of the play, and it is these which have been attributed by some to Shakespeare.

The popular play *Sir John Oldcastle* was at one time believed to have been written by Shakespeare. The title page of the first quarto printed in 1600 declares it to have been acted by the Lord Admiral's Men, and the title page of the second quarto (1619) actually has Shakespeare's name added as author. From evidence in the diary of Philip Henslowe, manager of the Admiral's Men, the play is now known to have been the combined effort of Michael Drayton and three of his contemporaries. The play appears to have been commissioned by the descendants of Sir John Oldcastle (the original of Falstaff) who thought their martyred ancestor had been slandered in Shakespeare's fat knight. The prologue announces: "It is no pampered glutton we present, / Nor aged Councellor to youthfull sinne," for in real life Sir John had been a renowned warrior, and the prologue more than hints that Shakespeare's depiction of the fat, bawdy knight is libelous.

The London Prodigall bears Shakespeare's name on the title page of the first edition (1605). Though it is a splendid comedy of London life, it is really unlike anything known to have been written by Shakespeare.

Sir John Oldcastle was once thought to have been written by Shakespeare.

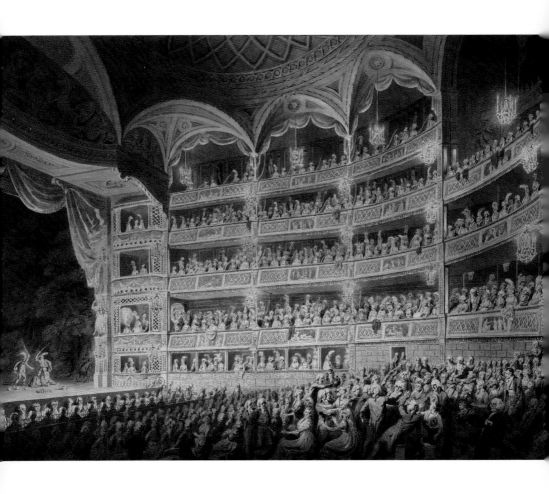

Drury Lane Theatre is the
oldest English theatre still
in use. It opened in 1663
and was managed by
Garrick from 1747 to 1776.

Bardolatry and Shakespeare Illustration

How far that little candle throws his beams!
—*THE MERCHANT OF VENICE* (5.1.90)

The first illustrated edition of Shakespeare appeared in 1709, edited by playwright and poet laureate Nicholas Rowe. It was based on the fourth folio and contained engravings by various artists. In 1736 a Shakespeare's Ladies Club was formed in London to stimulate interest in Shakespeare. A monument to Shakespeare was erected in Westminster Abbey in 1741. In 1765 Samuel Johnson published his edition of the plays, establishing the textual primacy of the First Folio. In 1750 the Drury Lane and Covent Garden theaters ran rival productions of *Romeo and Juliet*. More than a hundred years after Shakespeare's death, his reputation had weathered the Restoration and he was quickly becoming the brightest jewel in the crown of English literature.

Shakespeare performances in the eighteenth century were dominated by David Garrick (1717–1779). During his three decades at the Drury Lane Theatre, Garrick often reworked the plays in self-proclaimed pursuit of Shakespeare's intent. For instance, he restored to *King Lear* much of what Nahum Tate had expunged (see page 52). In 1769 Garrick helped organize a "Shakespeare Jubilee" in Stratford to celebrate the bicentenary of the poet's birth—albeit five years late. A major logistical undertaking, it generated strong responses—both positive and negative. Even though no Shakespeare play was performed and heavy rain on two of the three days forced cancellation of some events, it is considered the beginning of the Shakespeare industry that still thrives in Stratford; Jubilee tickets, programs, and other souvenirs from the event became valuable collector's items. In 1775 Garrick invited Sarah Siddons to perform with the company, and she became the most venerated of all Shakespearean actresses of her day. Like Garrick, Siddons was not only a talented performer, but a self-promoter who posed for many contemporary artists.

Souvenir ticket of admission for Garrick's 1769 Shakespeare Jubilee.

LEFT: David Garrick
dominated Shakespeare
performances in the
eighteenth century.

RIGHT: Sarah Siddons
was well known for her
portrayal of
Lady Macbeth.

In 1786, recognizing the poet's popularity, English engraver and publisher John Boydell and his colleagues announced an ambitious Shakespeare project which they hoped would lead to the founding of a British school of history painting. They commissioned two series of Shakespearean oil paintings—one large and one small—from all of the principal artists of the day. A gallery was built to exhibit the paintings and the paintings were published in two stunning printed works: One, a two-volume work, featured engravings of the large paintings, and the other, a folio edition, featured the text of the plays illustrated with engravings of the small paintings. Well-known critic George Steevens provided a new edition of the plays; a new style of type was designed and even a new ink created for what was envisioned as a new national edition of Shakespeare.

In 1789 Boydell opened his Shakespeare Gallery in Pall Mall, which quickly became a popular tourist destination for London visitors. As the paintings were finished, they were hung in the Shakespeare Gallery, which at one time contained 167 paintings by 33 artists. The publications took almost fourteen years to complete. The folio edition appeared in nine volumes, issued to subscribers in parts starting in 1791 and ending in 1805.

Just as Neoclassical Shakespeare supplanted Restoration Shakespeare, the eighteenth century gave way to the nineteenth and a Romantic Revival in which Shakespeare was exalted as a demigod. The Romantic Age in English literature begins in the late eighteenth century and traditionally ends in 1832 with the death of Sir Walter Scott and the passage of the First Reform Bill in Parliament. Of course, these beginning and ending dates are not absolute, and the literary attitudes characteristic of Romanticism began to emerge early in the eighteenth century (including reverence for Shakespeare), and extend through the Victorian era and into the twenti-eth and twenty-first centuries.

Engraved print from Boydell's landmark Shakespeare folio. Prints like this one from *A Midsummer's Night's Dream* (4.1) were engraved from full-size paintings.

THE EXTRA-ILLUSTRATED TURNER SHAKESPEARE

Henry Huntington was fascinated by extra-illustrated books, which were popular in Great Britain and the United States from the mid-eighteenth century to the early twentieth. The Library has about a thousand British and American extra-illustrated single volumes and sets. The book that started the craze, Richard Granger's *A Biographical History of England* (1769), ultimately gave its name to the practice. The word "grangerize" means to "extra illustrate." The Huntington holds the most ambitious extra-illustrated version of Granger's *History*, consisting of 35 volumes with 14,000 prints.

When putting together an extra-illustrated volume, collectors began with a book on a subject that interested them and gathered works of art, usually prints, to illustrate the text. The illustrations were mounted on sheets interleaved in the text and the book was rebound, often into several volumes. Although biography, history, travel, and the Bible were popular subjects for extra-illustrated books, editions of Shakespeare's plays were the most popular literary subject matter for extra-illustrating.

The Huntington has several extra-illustrated Shakespeares, the most ambitious of which is the one assembled by Thomas Turner of Gloucester. Beginning in 1835, Turner collected about three thousand prints and about seven hundred forty drawings and watercolors connected in some way with Shakespeare and his writings. The drawings range from fine examples by well-known artists to unimportant works by amateurs. The collection includes many depictions of Edmund Kean, the most famous actor of the early nineteenth century. Turner had these bound into a copy of John Boydell's 1802 edition of the plays, expanding it in the process to

LEFT: This engraved portrait of Thomas Turner is the frontispiece for each volume.

RIGHT: Title page for Turner's forty-four volumes of illustrations for Shakespeare's plays.

forty-four volumes. The plays are organized in the order in which they appear in the First Folio.

The Turner Shakespeare came into the collection in 1917 as part of the Bridgewater library and has been a resource to both Shakespeare scholars and students of British drawings. The volumes contain what is with little doubt the largest single accumulation of drawings connected with illustrated editions of Shakespeare from the eighteenth and early nineteenth centuries.

The Plays of William Shakespeare Illustrated by Thomas Turner, Esquire of Gloucester.

TOP: *The Comedy of Errors,* first printed in the First Folio, was based on Plautus's *Menaechmi,* but Shakespeare added a new pair of twins both named Dromio, pictured here. (5.1)

BOTTOM: Othello wrestles with Desdemona as she begs to be allowed to live just a little longer. (5.2)

The Virginia Steele
Scott Gallery of
American Art overlooks
the lush Shakespeare
Garden.

The Shakespeare Garden

There will we make our peds* of roses
And a thousand fragrant posies.
—*MERRY WIVES OF WINDSOR*, 3.1

*T*his informal garden, located between the Huntington and Virginia Steele Scott art galleries, is a version of an English landscape. It showcases plants mentioned in the bard's works, as well as other ornamental plants found in the gardens of the Elizabethan era. A streambed, filled with plants instead of water, courses through the center.

Pomegranate, rosemary, wild thyme, and garlic are some of the twenty or so plants marked with special plaques bearing botanical quotations from the works of Shakespeare. If you wander down the garden path, you'll also discover woodbine, grape, crab-apple, myrtle, sweet violet, lemon balm, fern, and holly.

A border of evergreen and flowering trees surrounds the garden, providing an elegant backdrop for the colorful display of blooming plants.

The Shakespeare garden is one of several at the Huntington that interprets plants in terms of culture and history. The others are the rose, herb, and Japanese gardens.

*natural soil aggregate

This bust of Shakespeare presides over the one-acre garden.

Endnotes

[1] Unless otherwise noted, all quotations from Shakespeare are taken from the *Riverside Shakespeare*, 2d ed., edited by G. Blackmore Evans et al. (Boston and New York: Houghton Mifflin, 1997). Full play titles are given with original spelling, punctuation, and capitalization, except that i/j and u/v are regularized as needed.

[2] In recent years Meisei University in Tokyo has amassed a dozen copies of the First Folio, making it the second-largest collection of that volume and the fifth-largest collection of rare and early editions of Shakespeare's works.

[3] The lot included Lodge's *Rosalynde* (1596), *Arden of Feversham* (1592), *King John, Parts 1 and 2* (1591), and Shakespeare's *The Rape of Lucrece* (1632), *Julius Caesar* (1684), and *Hamlet* (1676).

[4] For an account of the London address, see Samuel Schoenbaum, *William Shakespeare: Records and Images* (New York: Oxford University Press, 1981), 105–6.

[5] A Folger Shakespeare Library survey from the 1980s shows that Shakespeare is taught in 91% of U.S. high schools. The plays most often read are *Romeo and Juliet* (84% of schools), *Macbeth* (81%), *Hamlet* (51%), and *Julius Caesar* (42%).

[6] The manuscript is a part book for *Orlando* in Robert Greene's *Orlando Furioso* owned by Dulwich College in England. Alleyn founded the college.

[7] Along with Gilbert R. Redgrave, Pollard was the author of the first edition of *A Short-Title Catalogue of Books Printed in England, Scotland, & Ireland and of English Books Printed Abroad, 1475–1640*. Also known as the STC, the first edition, published in 1926, shows that Huntington's collection had three times as many STC entries as any other American library and ranked internationally only behind the British Museum and the Bodleian Library.

[8] The other plays printed for the first time in the First Folio are *All's Well That Ends Well, The Comedy of Errors, Coriolanus, Cymbeline, Henry VI Part 1, Henry VIII, King John, Timon of Athens, The Two Gentlemen of Verona,* and *The Winter's Tale.*

[9] *The Shakespeare First Folio: The History of the Book—Volume II: A New Worldwide Census of First Folios* by Anthony James West was published in 2003. The first volume of his massive study, *The Shakespeare First Folio*, was published by Oxford University Press in 2001. West has located 228 copies, 70 more than were listed in Sidney Lee's 1902 Census.

[10] *Ben Jonson*, ed. C. H. Herford and Percy and Evelyn Simpson, 6 (Oxford: Clarendon Press, 1938), 492.

[11] It is designated Q1; the first edition, also produced in 1598 but now existing only as a fragment, is called "Q0" (i.e., quarto zero).

[12] Thomas Jefferson, letter to Robert Skipwith, Monticello, 3 Aug. 1771, in Jefferson, *Writings*, ed. Merrill D. Peterson (New York: Library of America, 1984), 742.

[13] In a letter to Violet Hunt, 26 August 1903, James wrote: "I am 'a sort of' haunted by the conviction that the divine William is the biggest and most successful fraud ever practised on a patient world. The more I turn him round and round the more he so affects me. But that is all—I am not pretending to treat the question or carry it any further. It bristles with difficulties and I can only express my general sense by saying I find it almost as impossible to conceive that Bacon wrote the plays as to conceive that the man from Stratford, as we know the man from Stratford, did." *Letters of Henry James*, ed. Percy Lubbock [New York: Scribner, 1920], 1, 432.

OPPOSITE: *Twelfth Night.* Olivia unveils herself to Viola, who is disguised as Cesario. (1.5)

Bibliography

Blayney, Peter W. M. *The First Folio of Shakespeare.* Washington, D.C.: Folger Library Publications, 1991.

——. Introduction to *The First Folio of Shakespeare*, prepared by Charlton Hinman, 2d ed. New York: W. W. Norton, 1996.

——. *The Texts of King Lear and their Origins.* Vol. 1: *Nicholas Okes and the First Quarto.* Cambridge: Cambridge University Press, 1982.

Chute, Marchette. *Shakespeare of London.* New York: E. P. Dutton and Co., 1949.

Dickinson, Donald C. *Henry E. Huntington's Library of Libraries.* San Marino, Calif.: Henry E. Huntington Library and Art Gallery, 1995.

Duncan-Jones, Katherine. *Ungentle Shakespeare: Scenes from His Life.* London: The Arden Shakespeare, 2001.

Greenblatt, Stephen. *Will in the World.* New York: W.W. Norton and Company, Inc., 2004.

Holden, Anthony. *William Shakespeare: The Man Behind the Genius.* Boston: Little, Brown and Co., 1999.

Honan, Park. *Shakespeare: A Life.* Oxford: Oxford University Press, 1998.

Honigmann, E. A. J. *Shakespeare, The Lost Years.* Rev. ed. Manchester and New York: Manchester University Press, 1998.

McDonald, Russ. *The Bedford Companion to Shakespeare.* Boston: Bedford Books of St. Martin's Press, 1996.

Maguire, Laurie E. *Shakespearean Suspect Texts: The "Bad" Quartos and Their Contexts.* New York: Cambridge University Press, 1996.

A New History of Early English Drama. John D. Cox and David Scott Kastan, eds. New York: Columbia University Press, 1997.

Parish, William, and Dorothy Bowen. *William Shakespeare: An Exhibition Commemorating the Four Hundredth Anniversary of Shakespeare's Birth.* San Marino, Calif.: Henry E. Huntington Library and Art Gallery, 1964.

Private Libraries in Renaissance England: A Collection and Catalogue of Tudor and Early Stuart Book-Lists. R. J. Fehrenbach, gen. ed.; E. S. Leedham Green, U.K. ed. Binghamton, N.Y.: Medieval & Renaissance Texts & Studies; Marlborough, Eng.: Adam Matthew Publications, 1992.

Schoenbaum, Samuel. *Shakespeare His Life, His Language, His Theater.* New York: Signet, 1990.

——. *Shakespeare: The Globe & the World.* New York: Folger Shakespeare Library, and Oxford University Press, 1979.

——. *William Shakespeare: Records and Images.* New York: Oxford University Press, 1981.

Shakespeare, William. *Shakespeare's Plays in Quarto: A Facsimile Edition of Copies Primarily from the Henry E. Huntington Library.* Michael J. B. Allen and Kenneth Muir, eds. Berkeley: University of California Press, 1981.

Shattuck, Charles H. *Shakespeare on the American Stage.* [Washington]: Folger Shakespeare Library, 1976.

Sherbo, Arthur. *The Birth of Shakespeare Studies 1709–1821.* East Lansing, Mich.: Colleagues Press, 1986.

Taylor, Gary. *Reinventing Shakespeare: A Cultural History from the Restoration to the Present.* New York: Weidenfeld and Nicolson, 1989.

Thomson, Peter. *Shakespeare's Professional Career.* Cambridge. Cambridge University Press, 1992.

Wark, Robert R. *Drawings from the Turner Shakespeare.* San Marino, Calif.: Henry E. Huntington Library and Art Gallery, 1973.

Wells, Stanley. "Introduction" to *The History of King Lear.* Oxford: Clarendon Press, 2000.

——. *Shakespeare: A Dramatic Life.* London: Sinclair-Stevenson, 1994.

West, Anthony James. *The Shakespeare First Folio: The History of the Book.* Oxford: Oxford University Press, 2001.

SHAKESPEARE RESOURCES ON THE WEB

Bodleian Library
   http://www.bodley.ox.ac.uk/dept/scwmss/wmss/medieval/browse.htm
British Library
   http://www.bl.uk
Complete Works of William Shakespeare
   http://www-tech.mit.edu/Shakespeare/works.html
Early Modern Literary Studies
   http://www.shu.ac.uk/emls/emlshome.html
Electronic Text Center at the University of Virginia
   http://etext.lib.virginia.edu/shakespeare
Folger Shakespeare Library
   http://www.folger.edu
Furness Shakespeare Library at the University of Pennsylvania
   http://dewey.lib.upenn.edu/sceti/furness
Huntington Library Online Catalogue
   http://catalog.huntington.org
Internet Shakespeare Editions
   http://ise.uvic.ca
Mr. William Shakespeare and the Internet
   http://shakespeare.palomar.edu
Shakespeare Birthplace Trust
   http://www.shakespeare.org.uk
Shakespeare Electronic Archive
   http://shea.mit.edu
Shakespeare Illustrated
   http://shakespeare.emory.edu/illustrated_index.cfm
Shakespeare Magazine
   http://www.shakespearemag.com
Shakespeare Resource Center
   http://www.bardweb.net
Shakespeare's Globe
   http://shakespeares-globe.org

Caliban from *The Tempest*

List of Artists

All of the illustrations in *Not of an Age, but for All Time* are in the Huntington's extensive library and art collections. Many of these are drawn specifically from the Library's extra-illustrated Turner Shakespeare, which was nineteenth-century collector Thomas Turner's 44-volume scrapbook of Shakespeare's plays (for more on the Turner Shakespeare, see page 69). In order to illustrate specific scenes or characters, Turner supplemented Shakespeare's text with original art, often watercolors, as well as previously published woodcuts, paintings, and prints. Many of his volumes' original illustrations were commissioned from lesser-known artists, painted or drawn specifically for the project. Of these, we have emphasized the watercolors because, for the most part, they have not been seen outside the pages of the extra-illustrated volumes. Charming and colorful—though not necessarily well known—these vivid images reflect the popular tastes of the nineteenth century.

The Tempest (2.1), when Ariel prevents the murder of Alonso.

Falstaff speaks almost exclusively in prose through three plays: *Merry Wives of Windsor*, *Henry IV Part 1*, and *Henry IV Part 2*. The fat, funny knight has always been a favorite character. The old lecher is graced with wit, imagination, and vitality.

Acknowledgments

W hen a book finally appears in finished form after months and sometimes years of writing, rewriting, and research, it represents the work of many. This one is no exception, involving staff and volunteers from several Huntington departments.

We are grateful to the Rare Books staff, including Alan Jutzi, Stephen Tabor, and especially the department's pages who uncomplainingly brought out the huge Turner Shakespeare volumes as we needed them.

We also would like to acknowledge the excellent work of the Huntington Photographic Services Department, which was so careful and prompt in filling our reproduction requests. For help in searching for illustrations, we are especially grateful to Eileen Cole, a volunteer whose knowledge of library science and art history was enormously helpful, and to Genevieve Preston, Art Information Cataloger, who generously gave of her time to research possible Shakespeare illustrations among the Huntington's vast art holdings and to help us identify artists. We appreciate Carol Pearson's meticulous editing and attention to detail, which we hope has kept us from embarrassing oversights. Other behind-the-scenes activities included countless clerical tasks, for which we acknowledge the always cheerful and conscientious help of Sharee Wilkinson, a longtime Huntington volunteer.

The author wishes to thank the Huntington Library staff as well as several Shakespeare scholars who devoted their time, energy, and resources to this effort: Martha Andresen, Pomona College; A. R. Braunmuller, University of California, Los Angeles; Larry Green, University of Southern California; and Margaret Maurer, Colgate University. In addition, she wishes to thank friends and family who inspired and encouraged her, particularly Audrey Purcell, Ruth Bobo, and Mark and Jacob Edwards. Most especially, she wishes to thank Peggy Park Bernal, Director of Huntington Library Press, for engaging her in a project of all-consuming passion.

Shakespeare created many memorable female characters. Thomas Turner included these sentimental nineteenth-century color engravings in his extra-illustrated edition of the plays.

TOP: Ophelia (*Hamlet*)
MIDDLE FROM LEFT: Hero (*Much Ado About Nothing*), Cleopatra (*Antony and Cleopatra*), Katherine (*Taming of the Shrew*)
BOTTOM, FROM LEFT: Lady Anne (*Richard III*), Juliet (*Romeo and Juliet*)

Index

Illustrated pages are indicated by italic type.

Miniature of Queen Elizabeth I.

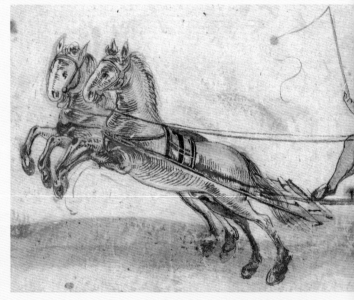